Team Spirit

THE CAROLINA PANTHERS

BY

MARK STEWART

Content Consultant
Jason Aikens
Collections Curator
The Professional Football Hall of Fame

NORWOOD HOUSE PRESS

CHICAGO, ILLINOIS

Norwood House Press
P.O. Box 316598
Chicago, Illinois 60631

For information regarding Norwood House Press, please visit our website at:
www.norwoodhousepress.com or call 866-565-2900.

PHOTO CREDITS:
All photos courtesy of AP Images—AP/Wide World Photos, Inc. except the following:
Streeter Lecka/Getty Images (cover);
Black Book Archives (7, 14, 20, 21 bottom, 23 top, 34 bottom left);
Topps, Inc. (34 bottom right & 40 top and bottom left).
Special thanks to Topps, Inc.

Editor: Mike Kennedy
Associate Editor: Brian Fitzgerald
Designer: Ron Jaffe
Project Management: Black Book Partners, LLC.
Special thanks to: Gloria Miller

LIBRARY OF CONGRESS CATALOGING-IN-PUBLICATION DATA

Stewart, Mark, 1960-
  The Carolina Panthers / by Mark Stewart ; content consultant Jason
Aikens.
    p. cm. -- (Team spirit)
  Summary: "Presents the history, accomplishments and key personalities of
the Carolina Panthers football team. Includes timelines, quotes, maps,
glossary and websites"--Provided by publisher.
  Includes bibliographical references and index.
  ISBN-13: 978-1-59953-130-4 (library edition : alk. paper)
  ISBN-10: 1-59953-130-5 (library edition : alk. paper)
  1. Carolina Panthers (Football team)--History--Juvenile literature. I.
Aikens, Jason. II. Title.
GV956.C27S74 2008
796.332'640975676--dc22
                                                    2007007474

Manufactured in the United States of America.

COVER PHOTO: Brad Hoover gets a hug from Jake Delhomme after a touchdown during the 2004 season.

Table of Contents

SPORTS WORDS & VOCABULARY WORDS: In this book, you will find many words that are new to you. You may also see familiar words used in new ways. The glossary on page 46 gives the meanings of football words, as well as "everyday" words that have special football meanings. These words appear in **bold type** throughout the book. The glossary on page 47 gives the meanings of vocabulary words that are not related to football. They appear in ***bold italic type*** throughout the book.

Meet the Panthers

There are many ways to win a game in the **National Football League (NFL)**. Some teams play rough and hit hard, hoping to *intimidate* their opponents. Other teams are fast and tricky, knowing they can defeat their opponents by catching them by surprise. The Carolina Panthers are a different kind of team. They win by keeping other teams from doing what they do best.

Carolina puts strong, smart players at each position. Every Panther is expected to contribute on the field, even if he is in the game for only a few plays. This makes the team very hard to beat.

This book tells the story of the Panthers. They are not a very old team, yet they have already experienced the sweet taste of victory. The players who wear the Carolina uniform are among the most confident in the NFL. If the Panthers keep the score close, the team and its fans believe they will find a way to win.

Ken Lucas and Chris Gamble celebrate an interception during the playoffs in January 2006. Carolina looks for talented and confident players who are great teammates.

Way Back When

The game of football has been popular in the states of North Carolina and South Carolina for almost 100 years. Some of the best players in history—including Sonny Jurgensen, Doc Blanchard, and Harry Carson—have come from this region. It was not until the late 1980s, however, that the NFL began to think about putting a team in this part of the United States. The person who convinced the league that there were enough fans in the Carolinas was Jerry Richardson. Richardson had played for the Baltimore Colts for two seasons and found great success in business after he left the NFL.

Richardson believed that the city of Charlotte, located in North Carolina near the border with South Carolina, was the *ideal* place for a new NFL team. He proved this when he got more than 40,000 fans to promise they would buy **season tickets**—in just a few days! The money Richardson collected went to build a new stadium for the Panthers, one of two **expansion clubs** that joined the NFL for the 1995 season.

The Panthers built their team by selecting unwanted players from other teams, **drafting** college stars, and signing **free agents**. The first player signed by the Panthers was Rod Smith, a speedy defensive back. Their quarterback was a **rookie** named Kerry Collins. One of the players **cut** in the team's first training camp was a **lineman** named Bill Goldberg. He went on to become a champion in **professional** wrestling. Carolina's first coach was Dom Capers. He had helped build a *dominant* defense for the Pittsburgh Steelers.

The 1995 Panthers were led by Sam Mills, who was a great linebacker and an *inspirational* leader. He returned an **interception** for a touchdown against the New York Jets to give the team its first victory. The Panthers won six more games in their first year, including four in a row. No expansion team had ever done that before.

In 1996, the Panthers added three important players: linebacker Kevin Greene, receiver Muhsin Muhammad, and tight end Wesley Walls. The team began the year with five wins and four losses. The fans were very happy. Defensive players Eric Davis and Lamar Lathon were playing especially well, as were Michael Bates and John Kasay, the stars of Carolina's special teams. Amazingly, the Panthers did not lose another game the rest of the regular season. They finished first in their division of the **National Football Conference (NFC)**.

The Panthers won their first **playoff game**, against the Dallas Cowboys. Suddenly they found themselves playing for the NFC Championship and a chance to go to the **Super Bowl**. Unfortunately, the Panthers lost to the Green Bay Packers. Soon, however, they began building a team good enough to win it all. It would not be easy, and there would be many ups and downs along the way, but they were determined not to let anything stop them.

LEFT: Sam Mills may have been small for a linebacker, but he made a lot of big plays.   **ABOVE**: Lamar Lathon slams into Troy Aikman of the Cowboys during Carolina's first playoff victory.

The Team Today

An NFL team is like a gigantic puzzle. To create a winning picture, a team needs all of its pieces on the table. Some years, the Panthers have not had all the right pieces, and they have fallen short of their goals. Other years, they have been just one or two pieces away from a championship.

When *assembling* their team, the Panthers look for a combination of experienced players and developing stars. On offense, they rely on strong runners and **blockers**, sure-handed receivers, and quarterbacks who are good leaders and build team spirit. On defense, Carolina likes fierce competitors and hard hitters. In recent years, the team's leaders included Jake Delhomme, Steve Smith, Julius Peppers, and Kris Jenkins.

The Panthers win games on the ground, in the air, and "in the trenches"—each week they try to find a new way to beat their opponent. During the season, the Panthers identify weaknesses in the teams they play and focus their strengths in these areas. After the season, they search for the pieces they need to complete the championship puzzle.

Nick Goings flashes a big smile as Steve Smith and Jake Delhomme congratulate each other after teaming up for a touchdown pass.

Home Turf

In their first season, the Panthers played in Memorial Stadium in Greenville, South Carolina. They shared it with the Clemson University football team. In 1996, the Panthers moved into a new home in Charlotte. At first, their field was called Ericsson Stadium. Later, its name was changed to Bank of America Stadium.

The Panthers' home field has a grass surface. Right beside the stadium are three practice fields—two are made of grass, and one is an artificial surface. When the team is preparing for a road game on artificial turf, the coaches make sure that the players get used to that surface during the week.

BY THE NUMBERS

- *There are 73,298 seats in the Panthers' stadium.*
- *The Panthers won the first game played on their home field, a 30–12 preseason victory over the Chicago Bears.*
- *The Panthers won their first two home playoff games—both against the Dallas Cowboys.*
- *In 2005, the Panthers retired number 51, which belonged to their beloved player and coach, Sam Mills. Mills had passed away earlier in the year.*

Panthers fans rise from their seats to watch the kickoff against the Chicago Bears in the first game ever played in Carolina's stadium, in 1996.

Dressed for Success

T he Panthers have worn the same team colors since joining the NFL in 1995. Their uniform features "Panther blue," silver, and black. The Panthers' helmet shows the head of a snarling panther. The team's *logo* is a full-length panther that is the same shape as the borders of North Carolina and South Carolina. Two stripes, designed to look like panther tails, begin at the front of the helmet and finish at the back of the helmet.

The Panthers wear two main jerseys—one is mostly black, and the other is mostly white. The team likes to wear white at home when the weather is warm, because this forces visiting teams to wear dark uniforms, which can get hot in the sun. The Panthers also occasionally wear a jersey in Panther blue.

The snarling panther can be seen on the helmet of Tommy Barnhardt, the team's punter in 1995.

The football uniform has three important parts—

- Helmet
- Jersey
- Pants

Helmets used to be made out of leather, and they did not have facemasks—ouch! Today, helmets are made of super-strong plastic. The uniform top, or jersey, is made of thick fabric. It fits snugly around a player so that tacklers cannot grab it and pull him down. The pants come down just over the knees.

There is a lot more to a football uniform than what you see on the outside. Air can be pumped inside the helmet to give it a snug, padded fit. The jersey covers shoulder pads, and sometimes a rib protector called a flak jacket. The pants include pads that protect the hips, thighs, *tailbone*, and knees.

Football teams have two sets of uniforms—one dark and one light. This makes it easier to tell two teams apart on the field. Almost all teams wear their dark uniforms at home and their light ones on the road.

The pads in DeAngelo Williams's pants are visible as he cuts sharply in a 2006 game.

We Won!

In 1996, in just their second season, the Panthers did the impossible when they won their division and reached the NFC Championship game. Over the next five years, however, the team failed to have another winning season. By 2002, the Panthers had become tired of losing and hired John Fox to coach the team.

Fox knew the Panthers already had good defensive players, including Mike Rucker, Kris Jenkins, Dan Morgan, Brentson Buckner, and Mike Minter. In the draft, the team added another star defender named Julius Peppers. The Panthers also had two very good receivers, Muhsin Muhammad and Steve Smith. What the team needed most was a powerful runner and a smart quarterback.

Prior to the 2003 season, the Panthers found both. The runner was Stephen Davis, a burly halfback who had led the NFC in rushing yards twice with the Washington Redskins. The quarterback was Jake Delhomme, who had tried to prove himself with the New Orleans Saints for five seasons without much success.

Davis gained 1,444 yards in his first year with the Panthers, while Delhomme won the starting quarterback job.

The Panthers won their first five games of 2003. Four of these victories came in close, exciting games. Two were won in **overtime**. Soon the players believed that they could beat anyone in the NFC. That included the mighty St. Louis Rams and Philadelphia Eagles. For most of the year, the experts were convinced that these two teams would meet for the NFC title.

The Panthers finished 11–5 and won the **NFC South** Division. They beat the Dallas Cowboys in the playoffs and then faced St. Louis. The Carolina defense played a great game, and Delhomme

guided the offense to two touchdowns and three **field goals**. The game was tied 23–23 at the end of 60 minutes. Neither team scored in the first overtime period. On the first play of the second overtime, Smith caught a pass from Delhomme and scored the winning touchdown.

Next, the Panthers traveled to Philadelphia to take on the Eagles. Both teams played excellent defense throughout the game. However, in the second quarter, Delhomme led a 79-yard **drive** to the end zone. Muhammad caught the final pass for a 24-yard touchdown.

A few minutes later, Rucker tackled Philadelphia quarterback Donovan McNabb very hard, badly bruising his ribs. McNabb struggled the rest of the game. In the second half, he threw two interceptions. The second led to a touchdown run by Panthers running back DeShaun Foster. Carolina went on to win 14–3. The Panthers were NFC champions in just their ninth season—and just two seasons after finishing 1–15.

Carolina's dream of winning the Super Bowl fell just short against the New England Patriots. In a thrilling game between the "Pats" and "Cats," the Panthers tied the game 29–29 with just over a minute left. The Patriots kicked a field goal as time ran out, however, and earned a 32–29 victory.

LEFT: The Panthers give coach John Fox a "victory shower" after the team's 2003 playoff victory over the Cowboys.   **ABOVE**: Julius Peppers congratulates DeShaun Foster on his touchdown against the Eagles.

Go-To Guys

To be a true star in the NFL, you need more than fast feet and a big body. You have to be a "go-to guy"—someone the coach wants on the field at the end of a big game. Panthers fans have had a lot to cheer about over the years, including these great stars …

THE PIONEERS

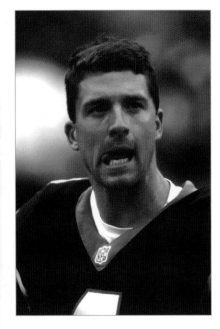

JOHN KASAY   Kicker

- BORN: 10/27/1969   • FIRST SEASON WITH TEAM: 1995

John Kasay joined Carolina in the team's first season and was the last of the "original" Panthers. In 1996, he set a new NFL record when he kicked 37 field goals.

SAM MILLS   Linebacker

- BORN: 6/3/1959   • DIED: 4/18/2005
- PLAYED FOR TEAM: 1995 TO 1997

Carolina needed an experienced leader in its first season, and Sam Mills was the perfect choice. He joined the team after nine great years with the New Orleans Saints. Mills was the only member of the Panthers to start every game in their first three seasons.

KEVIN GREENE   Linebacker

- BORN: 7/31/1962
- PLAYED FOR TEAM: 1996 & 1998 TO 1999

Kevin Greene was an "old man" of 33 when he joined the Panthers in 1996, but he played with the energy of a young boy. The joy Greene got from sacking the quarterback inspired the entire team.

MICHAEL BATES   Kick Returner

- BORN: 12/19/1969   • PLAYED FOR TEAM: 1996 TO 2000

It takes a special athlete to be a special-teams star in the NFL. Michael Bates won a *bronze medal* in the 200-meter dash at the 1992 *Olympics* and was honored as the NFL's best **kick returner** of the 1990s.

WESLEY WALLS   Tight End

- BORN: 3/26/1966   • PLAYED FOR TEAM: 1996 TO 2002

A tight end is expected to block on running plays, catch short passes, and hang on to the ball no matter how hard he is tackled. Wesley Walls did all three as well as anyone in the NFL. He was voted to the **Pro Bowl** five times as a member of the Panthers.

LEFT: John Kasay
TOP RIGHT: Kevin Greene
BOTTOM RIGHT: Wesley Walls

MODERN STARS

MUHSIN MUHAMMAD — Receiver

- BORN: 5/5/1973
- PLAYED FOR TEAM: 1996 TO 2004

Muhsin Muhammad was a tall, smart, and athletic receiver with a knack for making great catches. In 2004, Muhammad led all NFL receivers with 1,405 yards and 16 touchdowns.

MIKE RUCKER — Defensive End

- BORN: 2/28/1975
- FIRST SEASON WITH TEAM: 1999

Mike Rucker started just one game in his first two seasons with the Panthers. Once he got more playing time, he quickly became one of the NFL's best tacklers and toughest pass rushers.

DAN MORGAN — Linebacker

- BORN: 12/19/1978
- FIRST SEASON WITH TEAM: 2001

Dan Morgan was a college star who became a Pro Bowl linebacker after he joined the Panthers. Morgan was equally good at stopping running plays and passing plays.

LEFT: Dan Morgan
TOP RIGHT: Steve Smith
BOTTOM RIGHT: Julius Peppers

STEVE SMITH   Receiver

• BORN: 5/12/1979   • FIRST SEASON WITH TEAM: 2001

From the day Steve Smith joined the Panthers, he was one of the most exciting players in football. Fast and fearless, he returned punts and kickoffs, and then became one of the best receivers in the NFL. Smith caught 103 passes in 2005.

JULIUS PEPPERS   Defensive End

• BORN: 1/18/1980   • FIRST SEASON WITH TEAM: 2002

Many fans believe that Julius Peppers is the most talented player in team history. A running back in high school, he used his speed and agility to become one of the top defensive players in the NFL.

JAKE DELHOMME   Quarterback

• BORN: 1/10/1975   • FIRST SEASON WITH TEAM: 2003

Hardly anyone noticed when the Panthers signed Jake Delhomme in 2003. By the end of the season, he had led Carolina to the Super Bowl. Delhomme guided the Panthers to the playoffs again in 2005 and was voted to the Pro Bowl.

On the Sidelines

When a team is new to the NFL, it can take a long time to build a winning tradition. The Panthers have always believed that a positive attitude starts with a great coach and **front office**. When the team began play in 1995, it already had four winners on board.

The *majority owner*, Jerry Richardson, was a member of the 1959 NFL champion Baltimore Colts. The team's president, Mike McCormack, was a star for the Cleveland Browns during the 1950s. Bill Polian, Carolina's *general manager*, had an amazing eye for spotting talent. Head coach Dom Capers was a defensive genius.

The team's second coach, George Seifert, was also a winner. He had led his previous team, the San Francisco 49ers, to two Super Bowl victories. Carolina's next coach, John Fox, had been the defensive coordinator for the New York Giants when they won the 2000 NFC Championship. The Panthers were a one-win team when he took over. Two years later, they were playing for the NFL title. Fox was only the third coach in league history to accomplish this incredible feat.

Jerry Richardson and John Fox share a laugh during a Panthers practice.

One Great Day

During the 2003 season, no one could slow down the St. Louis Rams. When the Panthers met them in the playoffs that year, fans wondered whether Carolina's defense was good enough to stop the St. Louis offense. Few asked the more important question: Could the Rams stop the Panthers?

Starting in the second quarter, the Panthers scored on five **possessions** in a row. They led the game 23–12 with six minutes left, but the Rams came charging back. After scoring a touchdown and making a **two-point conversion**, St. Louis recovered an **onside kick**. Moments later, Jeff Wilkins booted the tying field goal.

The game went into overtime. The Panthers thought they had won after John Kasay kicked a field goal from 40 yards, but Carolina

was called for a penalty. Kasay had to try again from five yards back and missed his attempt. Next, the Rams had a chance to win, but Wilkins's kick from 53 yards away fell short.

Near the end of the first overtime, Ricky Manning Jr. of the Panthers intercepted a pass as the Rams were driving for the winning score. Two plays later, the referees whistled the end of the period. The exhausted players walked down to the other end of the field to start the second overtime. It was already the longest playoff game in NFC history!

On the first play of the second overtime, Jake Delhomme faded back and spotted Steve Smith slanting toward the middle of the field. He threw a quick pass that Smith caught near the 50 yard line. With an amazing burst of speed, he squirted between the two Rams trying to tackle him and made it all the way to the end zone. The crowd watched in stunned silence as the Panthers celebrated their sudden and spectacular 29–23 victory.

Legend Has It

Which Panther was named after two NBA Hall of Famers?

LEGEND HAS IT that Julius Peppers was. He was born Julius Frazier Peppers—named after basketball stars Julius Erving and Walt Frazier. Peppers was a great basketball player himself. Duke University basketball coach Mike Krzyzewski **recruited** him in high school. Peppers chose to attend the University of North Carolina because his hero, Michael Jordan, had gone there. In fact, only in college did he give up his dream of playing in the NBA and focus on the NFL. Peppers still loves basketball. Look closely on his left arm and you will see a tattoo of the Tasmanian Devil holding a football in one hand and a basketball in the other.

Julius Peppers's "Taz" tattoo is visible as he fights for a rebound during a college game.

Which Panther became an NFL star two seasons after breaking his neck?

LEGEND HAS IT that Steve Smith did. After being tackled on a punt return during a 1999 college game, Smith felt a strange tingle in his neck and shoulders. He played the rest of the game but was very lucky that he was not tackled hard again. That night, doctors placed Smith in a brace and **halo** for 10 weeks to **immobilize** his neck. They told him there was a good chance that he would never play football again. By 2001, Smith was fully recovered. He starred for the Panthers that season and was selected to play in the Pro Bowl.

Which Carolina quarterback once gave up football to play professional baseball?

LEGEND HAS IT that Chris Weinke did. In 1989, Weinke was rated as the best high-school quarterback in America. He claimed he was a better baseball player and signed a contract with the Toronto Blue Jays. He was wrong. Weinke played six seasons and never made it to the big leagues. He returned to football and won the Heisman Trophy as the nation's top college player in 2000. Weinke was Carolina's starting quarterback as a 29-year-old rookie the following season.

It Really Happened

E ver since the Panthers started playing in Charlotte, Catman has been sitting in the front row, behind the end zone in section 104. Everyone in town knows him. He is over six feet tall, weighs 340 pounds, and wears a blue wig that can be seen from the other side of the stadium. During the week, Catman is Greg Good, a counselor who works with troubled kids.

Carolina fans love Catman. They think of him as being part of the Panthers. They also don't like it when someone makes fun of him. David Hill, the head of the FOX Network, found this out in the summer of 2006.

During a Carolina preseason game that year, the announcers played a joke on Catman. After telling their audience that they planned to give a "new car" to a lucky fan, they presented a toy car to Catman. As it turned out, the joke did not go well—Panthers fans didn't think it was funny, and they protested to the network.

When Hill realized that a mistake had been made, he quickly flew to Charlotte. He presented Catman with the keys to a brand new pickup truck. "I'm grinning from ear to ear," said Catman after he climbed into the driver's seat, "because this time it's for real!"

LEFT: When the Panthers play at home, Greg Good becomes Catman.
ABOVE: Catman sits behind the wheel of his new truck, as David Hill looks on.

Team Spirit

Although the Panthers are still a young team, they have some of the NFL's most devoted fans. They are known for their fancy tailgate parties in the parking lot before kickoff, and many dress in Panther blue and silver for games. It took 75 years for the NFL to place a team in the Carolinas, and the fans want the league to know it was a great decision. They support their team by filling the stadium on Sundays and wearing the jerseys of their favorite players all year long.

Before the Panthers came to town, many people in the Carolinas rooted for the Washington Redskins. When the two teams play, it creates a lot of excitement. Panthers fans also get excited during games by the team's mascot, Sir Purr, and the TopCats dance team.

Today, the Panthers draw fans from all over the region. A look around the stadium parking lot shows cars with license plates from Georgia, Tennessee, Kentucky, West Virginia, Virginia, and, of course, North Carolina and South Carolina.

Jake Delhomme signs autographs for Carolina fans during a practice. The Panthers have fans from many different states.

Timeline

In this timeline, the NFC Championship is listed under the year it was played. Remember that the NFC Championship and the Super Bowl are held early in the year and are actually part of the previous season. For example, Super Bowl XLI was played on February 4th, 2007, but it was the championship of the 2006 season.

1995
The Panthers go 7–9 in their first season.

2001
Punter Todd Sauerbrun is named **All-Pro**.

1996
Kerry Collins leads the team to the NFC West title.

1997
The Panthers play in the NFC Championship game.

1999
Steve Beuerlein leads the NFL with 4,436 passing yards.

Kerry Collins

Steve Beuerlein

Ricky Manning Jr. celebrates an interception against the Eagles.

Brandon Short is the picture of joy after a 2006 playoff victory.

2004

The Panthers win the NFC Championship with a 14–3 victory over the Philadelphia Eagles.

2006

The Panthers reach the NFC Championship game for the third time.

2002

Julius Peppers is named Defensive Rookie of the Year.

2005

Steve Smith leads the NFL with 103 pass receptions.

Steve Smith

Fun Facts

LONG DISTANCE

The 85-yard touchdown pass from Jake Delhomme to Muhsin Muhammad in Super Bowl XXXVIII set a record for the longest play from **scrimmage** in Super Bowl history.

FEELING AT HOME

In 1995, the Panthers became the first major sports team to play its home games in South Carolina.

CUTTING IT CLOSE

The 2003 Panthers were nicknamed the "Cardiac Cats" because of their many heart-pounding victories. They tied two NFL marks by winning seven games by three points or fewer and three games in overtime.

I'LL SHOW YOU

During the 2005 playoffs, the Panthers beat the New York Giants 23–0. It was an especially satisfying victory for coach John Fox. He had once been in charge of the defense for the Giants.

FAN FAVORITE

Hardworking fullback Brad Hoover was one of Carolina's most beloved players. Whenever he made a good play, fans would chant, "HOOOOOOOOVER."

HERE KITTY

The Panthers are not the only "big cats" in North Carolina. The Charlotte Bobcats joined the NBA in 2004, and an earlier pro basketball team, the Carolina Cougars, played in the cities of Charlotte, Greensboro, and Raleigh. Also, the city bus system in Charlotte is called CATS (for Charlotte Area Transit System), and in Raleigh it is called CAT (for Capital Area Transit).

LEFT: Muhsin Muhammad celebrates his record-setting touchdown in Super Bowl XXXVIII. **ABOVE**: Brad Hoover

Talking Football

"I never had any doubts that
we would play in the Super Bowl."
—*Jerry Richardson, on building the Panthers
into a championship team*

"We play as a team and believe in
one another."
—*Dom Capers, on how the Panthers
became a winning team*

"You've got to win every week.
That's how the whole season is."
—*John Fox, on the pressures of
coaching in the NFC South*

"We are a team that is confident, but not a ***cocky*** football team."
—*Jake Delhomme, on what makes the
Panthers a winning team*

"If you hit the quarterback and the pass gets picked off, that's a lot better than a sack—you can't put all your stock in that category."

—*Mike Rucker, on the problem with judging a pass rusher only by his statistics*

"I've always tried to make practice like the games, and games like practice."

—*John Kasay, on how he prepares himself to kick in the NFL*

"I'd like to be the best. I want to be the best. I'm just going to do what I can to separate myself from everybody else."

—*Kris Jenkins, on what it takes to become an All-Pro*

"I've got all the tools. I just don't have the height!"

—*Steve Smith, who stands 5' 9" and caught 103 passes in 2005*

LEFT: Jerry Richardson **ABOVE**: John Kasay **RIGHT**: Kris Jenkins

For the Record

T he great Panthers teams and players have left their marks on the record books. These are the "best of the best" …

PANTHERS AWARD WINNERS

WINNER	AWARD	YEAR
Dom Capers	NFL Coach of the Year	1996
Julius Peppers	NFL Defensive Rookie of the Year*	2002
Steve Smith	NFL Comeback Player of the Year	2005

An award given to the league's best player in his first season.

Julius Peppers

Steve Smith

Dom Capers and Lamar Lathon flash big smiles after a victory during Carolina's amazing 1996 season.

PANTHERS ACHIEVEMENTS

ACHIEVEMENT	YEAR
NFC West Champions	1996
NFC South Champions	2003
NFC Champions	2003

RIGHT: Wesley Walls shouts to the Carolina fans after a Panthers playoff victory.
BELOW: Anthony Johnson races by Dallas defenders during the team's first postseason game, in 1996.

Pinpoints

The history of a football team is made up of many smaller stories. These stories take place all over the map—not just in the city a team calls "home." Match the pushpins on these maps to the Team Facts and you will begin to see the story of the Panthers unfold!

TEAM FACTS

1 Charlotte, North Carolina—*The Panthers have played here since 1996.*

2 Greenville, South Carolina—*The Panthers played here during their first season.*

3 Neptune, New Jersey—*Sam Mills was born here.*

4 Lebanon, Pennsylvania—*Kerry Collins was born here.*

5 Breaux Bridge, Louisiana—*Jake Delhomme was born here.*

6 Coral Springs, Florida—*Dan Morgan was born here.*

7 Cambridge, Ohio—*Dom Capers was born here.*

8 Ypsilanti, Michigan—*Kris Jenkins was born here.*

9 St. Joseph, Missouri—*Mike Rucker was born here.*

10 Tucson, Arizona—*Michael Bates was born here.*

11 Los Angeles, California—*Steve Smith was born here.*

12 Kinshasa, Democratic Republic of the Congo—
Tim Biakabutuka was born here.

Tim Biakabutuka

Play Ball

Football is a sport played by two teams on a field that is 100 yards long. The game is divided into four 15-minute quarters. Each team must have 11 players on the field at all times. The group that has the ball is called the offense. The group trying to keep the offense from moving the ball forward is called the defense.

A football game is made up of a series of "plays." Each play starts and ends with a referee's signal. A play begins when the center snaps the ball between his legs to the quarterback. The quarterback then gives the ball to a teammate, throws (or "passes") the ball to a teammate, or runs with the ball himself. The job of the defense is to tackle the player with the ball or stop the quarterback's pass. A play ends when the ball (or player holding the ball) is "down." The offense must move the ball forward at least 10 yards every four downs. If it fails to do so, the other team is given the ball. If the offense has not made 10 yards after three downs—and does not want to risk losing the ball—it can kick (or "punt") the ball to make the other team start from its own end of the field.

At each end of a football field is a goal line, which divides the field from the end zone. A team must run or pass the ball over the goal line to score a touchdown, which counts for six points. After scoring a touchdown, a team can try a short kick for one "extra point," or try again to run or pass across the goal line for two points. Teams can score three points from anywhere on the field by kicking the ball between the goal posts. This is called a field goal.

The defense can score two points if it tackles a player while he is in his own end zone. This is called a safety. The defense can also score points by taking the ball away from the offense and crossing the opposite goal line for a touchdown. The team with the most points after 60 minutes is the winner.

Football may seem like a very hard game to understand, but the more you play and watch football, the more "little things" you are likely to notice. The next time you are at a game, look for these plays:

PLAY LIST

BLITZ—A play where the defense sends extra tacklers after the quarterback. If the quarterback sees a blitz coming, he passes the ball quickly. If he does not, he can end up at the bottom of a very big pile!

DRAW—A play where the offense pretends it will pass the ball, and then gives it to a running back. If the offense can "draw" the defense to the quarterback and his receivers, the running back should have lots of room to run.

FLY PATTERN—A play where a team's fastest receiver is told to "fly" past the defensive backs for a long pass. Many long touchdowns are scored on this play.

SQUIB KICK—A play where the ball is kicked a short distance on purpose. A squib kick is used when the team kicking off does not want the other team's fastest player to catch the ball and run with it.

SWEEP—A play where the ball carrier follows a group of teammates moving sideways to "sweep" the defense out of the way. A good sweep gives the runner a chance to gain a lot of yards before he is tackled or forced out of bounds.

Glossary

ALL-PRO—An honor given to the best players at their position at the end of each season.

BLOCKERS—Players who protect the ball carrier with their bodies.

CUT—Removed from a team.

DRAFTING—Selecting players in the NFL's annual college draft.

DRIVE—A series of plays by the offense that "drives" the defense back toward its own goal line.

EXPANSION CLUBS—Teams added to a league when it grows.

FIELD GOALS—Goals from the field, kicked over the crossbar and between the goal posts. A field goal is worth three points.

FREE AGENTS—Players who are allowed to sign with any team that wants them.

FRONT OFFICE—The people who take care of a team's business matters.

INTERCEPTION—A pass that is caught by the defensive team.

KICK RETURNER—A player selected by his team to catch kickoffs and run them back.

LINEMAN—A player who begins each down crouched at the line of scrimmage.

NATIONAL FOOTBALL CONFERENCE (NFC)—One of two groups of teams that make up the National Football League. The winner of the NFC plays the winner of the American Football Conference (AFC) in the Super Bowl.

NATIONAL FOOTBALL LEAGUE (NFL)—The league that started in 1920 and is still operating today.

NFC SOUTH—A division for teams that play in the southern part of the country.

ONSIDE KICK—A short kickoff that the kicking team tries to recover.

OVERTIME—The extra period played when a game is tied after 60 minutes.

PLAYOFF GAME—A game played after the season to determine which teams play for the championship.

POSSESSIONS—The times a team's offense has the ball.

PRO BOWL—The NFL's all-star game, played after the Super Bowl.

PROFESSIONAL—A player or team that plays a sport for money. College players are not paid, so they are considered "amateurs."

ROOKIE—A player in his first season.

SCRIMMAGE—The spot on the field where the ball is placed to start each play.

SEASON TICKETS—Packages of tickets for each home game.

SUPER BOWL—The championship of football, played between the winners of the NFC and AFC.

TWO-POINT CONVERSION—A play following a touchdown where the offense tries to cross the goal line with the ball from the 2 yard line, instead of kicking an extra point.

ASSEMBLING—Putting together.

BRONZE MEDAL—The award for finishing in third place of an Olympic event.

COCKY—Sure of oneself in a rude way.

DOMINANT—Ruling or controlling.

GENERAL MANAGER—A person who oversees all parts of a company.

HALO—A metal device that keeps the head and neck still.

IDEAL—Appearing to be perfect.

IMMOBILIZE—Prevent from moving.

INSPIRATIONAL—Giving positive and confident feelings to others.

INTIMIDATE—Scare or frighten.

LOGO—A symbol or design that represents a company or team.

MAJORITY OWNER—The person among a group of owners who owns more than half of a company.

OLYMPICS—An international sports competition held every four years.

RECRUITED—Offered a college scholarship.

TAILBONE—The bone that protects the base of the spine.

Places to Go

CAROLINA PANTHERS
800 South Mint Street
Charlotte, North Carolina 28202
(704) 358-7000

THE PRO FOOTBALL HALL OF FAME
2121 George Halas Drive NW
Canton, Ohio 44708
(330) 456-8207

THE NATIONAL FOOTBALL LEAGUE   www.nfl.com
  • *Learn more about the National Football League*

THE CAROLINA PANTHERS   www.panthers.com
  • *Learn more about the Carolina Panthers*

THE PRO FOOTBALL HALL OF FAME   www.profootballhof.com
  • *Learn more about football's greatest players*

To learn more about the sport of football, look for these books at your library or bookstore:

  • Fleder, Rob–Editor. *The Football Book.* New York, NY: Sports Illustrated Books, 2005.

  • Kennedy, Mike. *Football.* Danbury, CT: Franklin Watts, 2003.

  • Savage, Jeff. *Play by Play Football.* Minneapolis, MN: Lerner Sports, 2004.

Index

PAGE NUMBERS IN **BOLD** REFER TO ILLUSTRATIONS.

The Team

MARK STEWART has written more than 20 books on football, and over 100 sports books for kids. He grew up in New York City during the 1960s rooting for the Giants and Jets, and now takes his two daughters, Mariah and Rachel, to watch them play in their home state of New Jersey. Mark comes from a family of writers. His grandfather was Sunday Editor of *The New York Times* and his mother was Articles Editor of *The Ladies' Home Journal* and *McCall's*. Mark has profiled hundreds of athletes over the last 20 years. He has also written several books about New York and New Jersey. Mark is a graduate of Duke University, with a degree in History. He lives with his daughters and wife Sarah overlooking Sandy Hook, New Jersey.

JASON AIKENS is the Collections Curator at the Pro Football Hall of Fame. He is responsible for the preservation of the Pro Football Hall of Fame's collection of artifacts and memorabilia and obtaining new donations of memorabilia from current players and NFL teams. Jason has a Bachelor of Arts in History from Michigan State University and a Master's in History from Western Michigan University where he concentrated on sports history. Jason has been working for the Pro Football Hall of Fame since 1997; before that he was an intern at the College Football Hall of Fame. Jason's family has roots in California and has been following the St. Louis Rams since their days in Los Angeles, California. He lives with his wife Cynthia and recent addition to the team Angelina in Canton, Ohio.

WITHDRAWN